# Perfect Freedom

Jane Williams is a tutor in theology at Trinity College Bristol and writes the 'Sunday Readings' column in the *Church Times*. Her husband is Rowan Williams, the Archbishop of Wales, and they have two children.

Other titles in the *Borders* series:

*Crossing Boundaries in Prayer*  Una Kroll
*Traffic in Truth: Exchanges between Science and Theology*  John Polkinghorne
*Living on the Border: Connecting Inner and Outer Worlds*  Esther de Waal

BORDERS

# Perfect Freedom

## Jane Williams

CANTERBURY
PRESS
Norwich

Text © Jane Williams 2001

First published in 2001 by The Canterbury Press Norwich
(a publishing imprint of Hymns Ancient & Modern Limited,
a registered charity)
St Mary's Works,
St Mary's Plain
Norwich, Norfolk NR3 3BH

British Library Cataloguing in Publication data

A catalogue record for this book is available
from the British Library

ISBN 1–85311–437–5

Typeset by Rowland Phototypesetting Ltd,
Bury St Edmunds, Suffolk
and printed in Great Britain by Biddles Ltd,
Guildford and King's Lynn

# CONTENTS

# SERIES INTRODUCTION

*The Borders series is published in association with the Society of the Sacred Cross, an Anglican religious community based at Ty Mawr, near Monmouth and close to the border between England and Wales.*

Visitors to the Society of the Sacred Cross at Ty Mawr, set in the hills south of the town of Monmouth, will be struck by the serenity and beauty of the place itself. The contemplative life of the Community is in tune with all that the place is and so, for successive generations of sisters, the land itself has been an integral part of their life. In former days they farmed the land themselves; when increasing age made this difficult, and then impossible, the farming of the land changed to helping in the care of lawns and flower-beds and sharing in the harvest of fruits. Yet to this day 'the land' remains focal, and in the recent exercise of renewal and rediscovery within the Society's life, the land has shared in the process, first in the reclaiming of the pond, originally the source of the House's water supply, then the planting of a coppice and now in the keeping of hens! The land then is seen as a metaphor of some of the new understandings now appearing.

Widely around Ty Mawr the land is marked with boundaries or borders of one kind or another. In one direction the town of Monmouth is on the border between England and Wales. Directly down into the valley in another direction is the village of Tintern, on the same river boundary with England and place of the splendid ruins of the medieval Abbey, so beloved of Wordsworth. In yet another direction is Chepstow with its great castle and site of the first of the two modern motorway bridges across the River Severn into England. Stretching away to the north is that strip of land called The Borders, rich in history and culture. The history is found in the line of castles along its length and is marked by a similar string of churches, some hidden amongst the hills like Patricio and Cwmyoy, others in more open country like Kil-peck and Abbey Dore. The culture is associated with names like Dom Augustine Baker, Henry Vaughan, Thomas Traherne, Arthur Machen and Philip Toynbee. For Ty Mawr there is significance too in the fact that all these borders lie on or astride the boundary between the two independent Anglican Church Provinces of Canterbury and Wales.

From all these there flows a host of ideas about meeting places, about thresholds, about situations of encounter. The interface between religious and secular, faith and science and the discovery that these meetings, frontiers or thresholds seldom end in 'either/or' so much as 'both/and'.

Traditionally Ty Mawr has been a place to which people have felt drawn, coming from a variety of worldly work or experience, sometimes from an already deeply committed faith in one Christian tradition or another, sometimes from another faith, sometimes even from no admitted faith at all, to find recovery of an inner serenity, a healing of wounds or the strengthening that comes from being apart for a while. Above all there has been the possibility to engage in that encounter with God which lies at the heart of the Christian way.

Out of the experience of the recurring natural

themes found in land and place and the Community's reflection on the experiences shared with all religious communities, there comes the title of this series – *Borders* books of encounter and exploration in which the reader is taken across a threshold to new insights, fresh understanding of things familiar and unfamiliar.

# PREFACE

An unpopular concept for our culture, mostly for very good reasons, is obedience. Yet it is inescapably central to Christianity, together with the intriguing notion that *only* in service to God can we be free.

The demand for 'obedience' has been used improperly over and over again in history. It has been used to keep slaves in subjection; it has been used as an excuse by torturers and executioners, who claim only to have been following orders; it has been used by men to define women.

But there has also, throughout the history of Christianity, been an undercurrent of creative obedience, exemplified not least by the monastic communities that continue to take vows of obedience. I think of the poet John Donne's great plea to God for freedom: 'For I, unless thou imprison me, never shall be free.' Donne, like the sisters of Ty Mawr, is acknowledging that there is no such thing as freedom. We are all constrained by something. The aim, then, is to choose what you will be obedient to, and to allow that obedience to free you more and more from other kinds of slavery. To belong to one Lord is to be freed from having to serve any others. And if the Lord you choose to serve happens to be God, then the biblical witness suggests that your slavery will lead to your becoming one of God's own children and heirs.

But, of course, the other side of that is that you cannot reach this state of freedom and grace without obedience. The hard, hard task is trying to be obedient to the true master, and resisting all the temptations to other kinds of slavery.

John Wesley once said that he preached his sermons because he needed to hear them, and that is the spirit in which I am writing this book. I am not a naturally rebellious person, but I have been made aware, in all kinds of areas of my life, that unthinking obedience to the way things are is not necessarily obedience to God. In particular, as a woman deeply indebted to the feminist movement, I have noticed that it is easy to cite 'obedience' and ignore God's particular, demanding call to me as an individual. Letting someone else make decisions for you is not the same as obedience.

In what follows, I want, first, to tell you a little about the particular circumstances out of which this book arose, and then to look at Jesus, the model of Christian obedience, and finally to try to apply that model to some of the hard cases we have to face, where it is not clear what obedience might mean. I hope the end result might be a bit more clarity about whose service we are in, and what kind of freedom that offers us.

# 1

## A PERSONAL PARADOX

In 1992 my husband was elected Bishop of Monmouth, in the Anglican Province of Wales.

Until that point, I had assumed that, although he was ordained, his primary vocation was to academic life. We were living in Oxford, where he was a professor of theology, and a canon of Oxford's cathedral, Christ Church. A medieval eleven-bedroomed house in the cloister of the college went with the job, together with a huge and magical garden, where our small daughter and I spent many happy hours, and where I constantly expected to see the Cheshire Cat grinning at me from the branches of the seventeenth-century plane tree.

So it is only honest to admit that my reluctance to move to Wales was at least in part because of having to leave behind a comfortable and privileged lifestyle.

To be Bishop of Monmouth, my husband would accept a considerable drop in income and an ugly modern house in what seemed to me a decaying part of a town that history had left behind. I remember going to have a sneak-preview of Newport one Saturday afternoon, before the decision was final. Walking through a town that seemed knee-deep in McDonald's wrappers, and apparently with nowhere but a Wimpy to have a cup of tea, I had a deep psychic certainty that we would never live in this place. So much for psychic certainty. (Of course, it is only fair to say that Oxford is usually knee-deep in McDonald's wrappers by Saturday afternoon as well, and though it may have huge numbers of wonderful cafés, you cannot usually get into them for the tourists, but I chose not to recall any of that on my first, gloomy, walk round Newport.)

But if selfishness and materialism played a large part in my first reaction to the call to Wales, so did a sense of what my husband was actually doing in Oxford. As a highly intelligent priest and gifted teacher, he was clearly holding open the door to many students, enabling them to see a way of being both orthodox and intelligent. Looking round the

Anglican Church, it is interesting to note how many of those students are now doing the same kind of job for others. This seemed to me then, and still seems to me now, a genuine vocation.

But my husband was convinced that God was actually calling him to a different kind of service, one that was more directly priestly, or churchy, if you like, but also more incarnational. It is very, very hard for a Christian spouse to say 'No' to a partner's sense of God's calling. Although I am fairly sure that if I had refused to contemplate the move, we would not have made it, I did not quite have the courage to do that. After all, what if it really was God's calling?

So, in the early summer of 1992, we moved to Newport, and our day-to-day lives changed dramatically. My daughter went to the wonderful but far from middle-class local school, and quickly learned a broad Newport accent for school use. It put her in a real quandary when we walked home with school friends, because she had to decide whether to use her school voice for them, or her home voice for me.

My husband's life became instantly far less family-friendly. Instead of academic terms, which were totally all-consuming for eight weeks, but then relaxed at roughly the same time as school holidays, his diary became uniformly full, with particular bursts of busyness in the Easter and Christmas school breaks. He also found that he was out most evenings, instead of being around to help with bath-time. My catering standards came under enormous pressure in our new life. My husband's natural style is to combine some less formal meetings with hospitality; he used to be able to take guests in to dine in Hall, but now he has to forage hopefully in the kitchen. I blush to think of the number of people who have eaten plain cheese sandwiches in my untidy kitchen, which may not have been what they were expecting when invited to lunch with the bishop!

My immediate way of avoiding being a bishop's wife, for which I felt that I had no calling, was to look for a job, and I have been fortunate enough to find two of the nicest jobs a person could ever ask for. First of all, I worked for a religious publishing firm, which I loved. I got to read some very interesting books, and talk to some wonderful people, I had lovely colleagues, and I was even earning money. Perhaps this move to Wales was, after all, a blessing in disguise?

But then, wholly unexpectedly, I discovered myself to be pregnant again, having long ago reconciled myself to having just the one – completely perfect – daughter. I was not best pleased, to put it mildly. Kicking and struggling, I realised that I would have to give up my glorious career, since commuting to London and working full-time would clearly leave no time at all to be a mother.

It was my husband who drew my attention to an advertisement in the *Church Times* for a tutor at Trinity College Bristol. Bristol was a far more realistic commute, and the job was, in any case, part-time, so I applied, got the job and am still amazed at my good fortune. It is, if possible, an even better job, with the added advantage of fitting in well with the children's school holidays. And the baby turns out to be spectacular, too. So now I'm waiting for the next surprise (no, no, I don't really mean it, Lord!). I feel that I have been enormously rewarded for a very small and grudging step into obedience. I took that step, not because my husband demanded it of me – he didn't. That is not the kind of obedience I am talking about.

It was partly out of obedience to his vision of God's calling, and it was a vision that I could, though very reluctantly, see matched with what the Bible tells us about what God is like. The call to Abraham, or to the Exodus people of Israel, was a call to step out in faith, towards a vision of a community based on God. This is the call to the Church, too. It is above all a call to imitate Jesus, to be, through the Holy Spirit, the people where God is made visible, who trust in nothing but God, who are held together by no other ties.

It was also partly out of obedience to a vision that God gives in marriage. When we get married, we commit ourselves to learning and growing *together*, in the belief that, for those who are called to marriage, God makes the learning together into something far bigger than either could learn alone. The faithfulness and commitment that are essential to a marriage are signs of God's enormous faithfulness towards us, his creation, and you cannot expect such signs to work only when everything is easy and straightforward. You hardly need to use words like 'faithfulness and commitment' if there are no disagreements, no testings. It is clear that not all married couples can or should stay together, if the marriage is actually destructive, but it does frighten me that people give up at the first sign of struggle nowadays. And not just in marriage, but in anything. Where would we be if God took that attitude?

So it was partly obedience to this vision of myself-in-relation, myself as one part of an organic and growing whole, myself, if you like, in trinitarian terms, that led me to agree to the move to Wales.

I cannot promise that obedience always leads to happiness and prosperity, but I think I will risk promising that obedience, if it is actually obedience to God's calling, will always lead to growth, and when we stop growing, we die.

The big question, of course, is how we know what is obedience to *God's* calling. Certainty is the great luxury that is often denied to Christians. Although I may sound certain on the page, I was not at all certain for several years after we made the move that this really was of God. And sometimes, still, when I see how wearing the job of being a bishop is, and how much of it seems to be generated by the sheer stupidity of the Church, and how few signs of growth or of the Spirit there are, day by day, I look back wistfully to the heady days of academic freedom, when we could almost hear the students lapping up wisdom and giving us love in return. I suppose I am now reasonably certain that we are where God has called us to be, for the moment, although I cannot help thinking that God does have some very strange ideas.

But then I suppose I knew that already. After all, he does not ask what he does not do himself. I am, of course, talking about the Incarnation, and it is to that that I turn next.

# 2

## THE OBEDIENCE OF CHRIST

### *The Kingdom of God*

The New Testament tells us that one of the most characteristic things about Jesus' mission was his proclamation of the Kingdom of God. In Mark's Gospel, the first words we hear Jesus speak are 'The time is fulfilled, and the kingdom of God has come near' (1:15). But what is 'the kingdom of God'? At its most basic, it is surely the place where God is obeyed, where his rule is acknowledged and accepted. As the gospel stories progress, it becomes clearer and clearer in all four Gospels that Jesus is aware of some necessary connection between his own mission and the Kingdom of God, and that people's reaction to him *is* their reaction to the proclamation of God's rule. Some of the people that Jesus meets see God's rule as threatening their own autonomy or their own power base, and the Gospels tell us that it is often the religious people who actually do not want to acknowledge the direct rule of God. They want to keep God confined in religious rules and observances, rather than be faced with God himself, with his direct and personal demands upon them.

Other people, the Gospels tell us, meet the reign of God with relief and joy, and they tend to be the people who are being oppressed and downtrodden by human rule. So the poor, the outcast, the sick and women tend to be the ones who see that God's reign will be liberating for them. They see that they will be given the chance to start afresh, rather than being marked as failures, losers and lawbreakers, often from birth, by circumstances completely outside their own control.

It is easy and, of course, true, to see Jesus as someone with extraordinary authority and power. The miracles stories and the teaching, often given in humorous and idiosyncratic stories, are recognized by the gospel writers as full of power. But what is equally striking is that Jesus nearly always speaks of this power as delegated to him. There are a couple of stories that bring this point out very clearly. The first is the story of the Roman centurion who asks Jesus to heal his slave (Luke 7:2–10). The centurion says a very odd thing to Jesus: 'I also am a man set under authority, with soldiers under me; and I say to one "Go", and he goes, and to another "Come" and he comes.' Jesus praises this centurion more warmly than almost anyone else in the Gospels. Now notice that the centurion knows that Jesus' authority, like his own, is based on the fact that he is himself *under* the authority of another. The centurion's authority comes from the fact that he holds command in the Roman army, and is a symbol of its might; and he has recognized the fact that Jesus' authority, too, is delegated, in Jesus' case from God.

So it may well be that Jesus is an attractive and powerful personality – the reaction of those who meet him in the Gospels would seem to confirm that – but his personality is not the source of his authority – God is.

Another story, this time one of Jesus' own stories, makes the same point. It is the story of the vineyard owner whose unruly tenants attempt to keep possession of the vineyard (Mark 12:1–12). He sends slaves to regain the property, but they are abused, so finally he sends his son and heir. But the tenants recognize him and know his claim on the property and they kill him.

This story comes in Mark's Gospel as part of the build up to the crucifixion. In Mark 11 Jesus enters Jerusalem, and the scene is set. What follows is a series of confrontations with the religious authorities, whose constant question is 'Who do you think you are?' It is directly in response to the question 'By what authority are you doing these things?' (11:28) that Jesus tells the terrible parable of the vineyard owner. His listeners surely could not have missed the point. Not only is Jesus claiming to be the son of the 'owner', but also he is saying, quite pointedly, that the chief priests, scribes and elders *know* who he is, and that is why they oppose him. Just as the tenants hope to keep the property by killing the heir, so the authorities hope to keep power over the people by breaking Jesus' power.

So, clearly, Jesus is claiming to exercise the authority of God. He is claiming to be God's delegate, with the right to interpret God's laws. But the point of his ministry is not that people should acknowledge his authority and submit to it, but that they should recognize the God who sent him. Mark's Gospel makes this clearest, with what has often been called the 'messianic secret'. In Mark's Gospel, Jesus is often found telling people to keep quiet about who has healed them. So, for example, in Mark 1:43, when Jesus heals the leper, he tells the man to go to the priest and get his healing verified, but not to say how it happened. All kinds of explanations have been offered for this 'secretiveness' of Jesus, but it looks as though at least part of the explanation is that Jesus wants the work of God acknowledged as precisely that. He does not want to set up a personality cult, but to bring others to worship God and to acknowledge God's sovereignty.

## 'He Humbled Himself'

The Christian recognition of Jesus as God incarnate is, paradoxically, based on just this fact – that Jesus does not claim to be God. He acts, speaks, lives, dies and rises as one who has totally submitted himself to the God whom he called Father, and it is this total submission that marks him out from the rest of us. What other historical figure has had such power, such effect, and yet has spent their whole time pointing away from themselves? The Gospels clearly show us that Jesus spent a lot of his time trying to get away from people's expectations and projections. People saw his power and wanted him to be king, to solve all their problems, to change everything, to take up arms. Even his own disciples, who must have been most exposed to his teaching and his sense of calling, did not understand what he was about, but longed to share in his power. Mark 10:35ff. tells the story of how James and John, two of the disciples at the heart of Jesus' mission, come to him and ask him if they can sit on either side of him in his glory. Jesus tries hard to reinterpret their request in terms of his own understanding of his mission of suffering and death, but you get the feeling that his disciples have no clue what he is talking about. And yet this is really quite late on in Jesus' hectic mission, almost immediately before the entry into Jerusalem, which is to build up into the passion narrative. These are disciples who, according to Mark, have constantly witnessed Jesus' attempts to deflect attention away from himself, but yet they are still obsessed with power. It seems that these concepts of obedience and relinquishment of power are the hardest things of all for the disciples – and us – to grasp.

In Philippians 2:5–11 Paul has a profound meditation which moves us on a stage further in our exploration of obedience. Paul suggests that it is because Christ was prepared to be humbled, 'taking the form of a slave, being born in human likeness', that he is exalted and made worthy of worship. The one who is God, but is prepared to be seen as nothing, is the one whom we can now recognize as the revelation of God.

Although this seems strange, it actually makes perfect sense. Paul wants his readers to see the paradox, because he wants them to take a fresh look at their own attitudes, and to think about obedience to a bigger vision. He is trying to encourage the Philippians to think about themselves as a community, putting the interests of others before their own. It is, I feel, rather encouraging that this anti-individualistic message needed to be heard almost two thousand years ago. It seems that it is not only Western materialists who suffer from self-absorption.

But if we remember that the heart of Jesus' mission is to proclaim the Kingdom of God, it makes perfect sense that the one who proclaims should be the one who demonstrates. The Kingdom of God, we have suggested, is the place where God is obeyed, where his laws and his rule are recognized. It is surely vital that the one who preaches the closeness of the Kingdom should demonstrate it in his own life. In the life, death and resurrection of Jesus, we know that the Kingdom of God is indeed present, because here, as nowhere else, God is obeyed. Everything Jesus says, does and is comes out of obedience to God, the Father. So it is no surprise that he constantly deflects questions about his own status and authority. To those who have eyes to see and a mind to understand, the fact of his obedience speaks for itself. Nowhere else, as Paul so poignantly points out in Romans, has such obedience been found. Although the Law sets out what is required for obedience to God, no one can actually keep the Law. So the total obedience to God that we see in Jesus is unique. Only one utterly in tune with God's own nature is capable of such obedience.

## *Obedience Christology*

The German theologian Wolfhart Pannenberg has made this the basis of his Christology. In his complex and influential book *Jesus – God and Man*, he is trying to look at Jesus without the presuppositions that we now inevitably bring to such a study. He is trying to get us to see the *historical* Jesus, just as Jesus' own contemporaries would have seen him, so that we can try to grasp how it came about that, so soon after his death, people began to make such enormous claims about who Jesus is, and how he relates to the Father. This is called doing Christology 'from below', starting with the observable, historical human being, rather than 'from above', with the descent of the second person of the Trinity into the human world. It is attempting to start with an ordinary human view, rather than with the knowledge that hindsight and centuries of Christian interpretation bring.

Pannenberg's argument works on a number of different levels, and we do not need to concern ourselves with all of them in this discussion. For our purposes, what is significant is that Pannenberg recognizes obedience as one of the clues to the real identity of Jesus. 'The man Jesus . . . lived in dependence on the Father, but precisely in so doing showed himself to be one with the Son.'[1] This is doctrinally a very exciting idea. The problem that has usually dogged Christian discussion of the Incarnation is how you can get godhead and humanity into one person without impairing either of them or mixing them up into something that is neither divine nor quite human. The classic definition of Christology, produced at the Council of Chalcedon in 451, tells us simply that godhead and humanity *do* coexist in Jesus, and that neither is changed, or confused with the other, yet at the same time, the human person of Jesus is not divided or separated. But although this is acknowledged as the definitive goal which all christological statements must reach, it gives us no imaginative or pictorial clues as to how to see Jesus in this way.

What Pannenberg is suggesting is beautifully simple, and bears all the hallmarks of God's own humorous and faithful purposes. Instead of looking at Jesus for all the marks of what we commonly mean by divinity – such as omnipotence, omniscience and general works of astounding power, we are instructed to look at Jesus for what are properly the characteristics of humanity. So we look at Jesus and see someone vulnerable, someone who suffers and dies, someone who knows himself to be subject to his maker, called to do God's will, even when he does not entirely understand it, someone who has to struggle to understand his own vocation.

These things are part of the human condition as we know it, yet most of us are constantly fighting against them, and trying to make ourselves invulnerable, and to claim total control over our own lives. We are trying, in other words, to be like our image of God. Jesus, on the contrary, is being what we are created to be. And because Jesus accepts his fate and is totally obedient to God, he is actually mirroring God, as we should. The Genesis theology of creation tells us that human beings are made 'in the image of God', and that it is only our willingness to be mirrors, not the primary image, that gives us authority in creation (Genesis 1:26f.). Authority derives from obedience.

This is shown most clearly in the life of Jesus. It is because he acts always in submission to God that he is able to teach and heal and forgive sins 'with authority'. It is because he is willing to be just a human being, as few human beings are willing, that he is able to be the source of our new creation. We were not able to accept the terms of our original creation, and constantly strove to be gods instead of human. Jesus, who actually is God, is content to exercise authority in God's name, rather than his own, and in so doing recreates God's original idea. This is the source of Paul's analogy of the first and last Adam. Jesus is the 'new humanity', who is also what God originally intended humanity to be.

The extraordinary logical consequence of this line of thinking is that, had humanity been prepared to be 'in the image of God', as we were intended to be, we could have been 'divine', as Jesus is! But God, in his enormous and creative power, is not thrown off course by our disobedience. Instead, what should have been ours by right of our created nature is made ours by grace of our recreated nature in Jesus. We can still be 'divine', we can still be the image of God, as Jesus was, by accepting the place that he now holds open for us, by becoming his 'body'.

## *Learning Obedience in the Body of Christ*

But although this is theologically and imaginatively a helpful set of clues, how does it further our own Christian discipleship of obedience? If we acknowledge that we are called to be 'the body of Christ', and so to be the new creation, the Kingdom of God, where God's rule is accepted with gladness, how do we set about this?

If we turn again to Jesus, we find that this 'obedience' is not a simple thing. We see, first of all, that Jesus had to grow into his mission. He had to work at how he was to be obedient to the Father. The gospel writers give us tantalizingly few clues about Jesus' own sense of himself, his consciousness. What they do say suggests that Jesus had a strong sense, from early on, that he was called to proclaim the Kingdom of God, and that there was some kind of direct relationship between himself and what he was teaching.

But beyond that, Jesus had to test each step, as far as we can tell. All the Gospels agree that Jesus' mission begins with his baptism by John the Baptist, and that this marks some kind of a realisation of where he was going. Matthew and Luke flesh this out with the telling of Jesus' temptation in the wilderness (Matthew 4:1–11; Luke 4:1–3). These stories explore ideas of power and obedience, and show Jesus coming to an articulation of the fact that the power he is to exercise is not for his own benefit, and is not to be seen as his own power. It is highly significant that this time of tempting comes directly after Jesus' baptism. The whole direction of his ministry is being determined. The temptation to power and success come as soon as his ministry is confirmed.

Jesus makes the decision that Adam and Eve failed to make, and he answers the devil as they should have answered the serpent in Eden. 'Worship the Lord your God, and serve only him,' he says in Matthew. Or 'Do not put the Lord your God to the test,' in Luke.

## The Disobedience of Christ

But this is not the end of the matter. The choice of obedience to God has to be made over and over again in Jesus' ministry. At the wedding in Cana (John 2:1–11), Jesus' mother is making a bid for fame for her son, one that she has to learn, with bitterness, that he will not back up. All the Gospels show a tension between Jesus and his family, in which they seem to be demanding his obedience to family, while he has chosen an obedience to God that brings him into inevitable conflict with his family.

And yet, families are not *bad*. Most societies recognize families as the basic unit, and see the proper working of families as the glue that holds the community together. Jesus' calling to mission is one that runs counter to what were and are generally accepted rules. In other words, his obedience must have *looked like disobedience* to his contemporaries.

The same thing happens, so the Gospels tell us, in his relations with the religious norms of his society. Jesus honours the Law by breaking it. In other words, his radical obedience to what he saw as the *spirit* and intention of the Law often involved him in breaking the actual day-to-day rules which were accepted by his peers as the best interpretation of the Law. Look, for example, at the stories about the Sabbath. Jesus heals on the Sabbath, he allows his followers to pick wheat to eat on the Sabbath, and so on. All of these are hotly questioned by the 'Pharisees', who represent the most devout section of the population, and who are trying to live their lives in obedience to God, through obeying the Law. It is easy to forget, in reading the Gospels, that the Pharisees did not set out to be the villains of the piece. They saw Jesus as directly challenging the Law which governs the proper relationship between God and his people. In other words, they saw Jesus as *disobedient*.

Jesus' cleansing of the Temple stands at the heart of the problem for this exploration of Jesus as God's obedient servant. I do not see how any devout Jew could have seen that action as one of obedience to God. Even if they agreed that the commercialization of the Temple was a mistake, the violence of Jesus' reaction must have been a shock. And the underlying message, that Jesus had the authority to judge what God's reaction to this would be, is the source of the tension between Jesus and his Jewish critics. It looks like a kind of assertion of individual autonomy over and against the collective and inherited understanding of the will of God.

This was clearly not an easy choice on Jesus' part. There are all kinds of incidents in the Gospels that show us the depth of Jesus' commitment to Israel. Think of his response to the Syrophoenician woman;

think of the way in which he weeps over Jerusalem as he enters it on his way to death. Think of his knowledge of and love of the Scriptures. To stand against his religious community is not an easy choice for Jesus.

Think, too, how lonely Jesus' path of obedience was. His obedience to his heavenly Father has cost him acceptance by his family and by his religious community. Admittedly, it has brought him followers and admirers, but even they cannot understand what is driving him. Many people obviously followed Jesus simply for the miracles. Some are intrigued by the teaching, catching glimpses of something that attracts them and makes them long for God. His closest friends, even, have not understood that Jesus' mission is not about power but about submission.

Their mistake is understandable, given the undoubted power that they saw and heard Jesus exercising. They heard the extraordinary and gripping teaching; they saw the miracles, and were occasionally even able to perform them themselves. They also glimpsed, the Gospels suggest, that Jesus' mission was something to do with re-establishing God's rule over Israel. But some of them, at least, seem to have thought of that in political terms, so that they were looking for the overthrow of Roman rule, and the reign of God's Messiah, Jesus. They had high hopes of what might be offered to the disciples of the Messiah. Although the Gospels show us that Jesus tried, time and time again, to warn his followers about the end result of his mission, and to get them to rethink what God's reign might mean, they just could not grasp it. And do you honestly think you would have done, in their place?

It is tempting to think that this constant struggling against the expectations of those around him was made easy for Jesus by his clear conviction of what God had called him to. Surely obedience for Jesus was easy, because he heard God clearly, all the time, giving instructions and approving what Jesus was doing?

The Gospels do suggest that Jesus was driven by overwhelming conviction, and that, even at the most frenetic times in his ministry, he withdrew to be quiet and listen to God. But they also suggest that even Jesus could not always be absolutely certain that he had got it right. We are told that, in the garden of Gethsemane, as Jesus waits for the death he has been predicting and warning his followers about for so long, he longs for another outcome. 'My Father, if it is possible, let this cup pass from me; yet not what I want but what you want' (Matthew 26:39), he prays. This acknowledgement, at this most fraught moment, that there is a distinction between what Jesus wants and what God wants, is almost unbearably poignant. It is, we believe, part of Jesus' genuine identification with our human situation that for him, as for us, obedience to God is not easy, it does not overrule the natural human desires and replace them with God's own view of things.

Even more telling is Jesus' cry of dereliction on the cross. Matthew and Mark report that Jesus cried, in his dying agony, 'My God, my God, why have you forsaken me?' (Matthew 27:46; Mark 15:34). All the certainty that had driven his mission to this point was not enough. At this point of terrible agony, Jesus' sense of obedience seems swallowed up in the feeling that God has not honoured that obedience, that God has gone away. And if God had indeed deserted him, then his whole mission is called into question. Perhaps he was wrong. Perhaps he had not been being obedient to God. Perhaps those who had seen him as a law-breaker and a blasphemer were right.

Now, of course, we know the rest of the story. We know that in the resurrection God does indeed honour Jesus, and acclaim his mission as one of true obedience to the will of God, obedience, indeed, that is life-giving for others. But the story of Gethsemane and of the cry from the cross show us beyond doubt that obedience to God is not easy, and that *no one, not even God's own Son*, can have the constant luxury of *knowing* that they are obedient. To strive for obedience to God does not take away the human necessity of struggling, growing, making mistakes, facing uncertainty. Jesus' obedience shows us that is proper. We should not expect always to be held in peace and serenity because we are trying to do God's will.

Jesus also shows us that living in the Kingdom of God, that is, creating places and people where God is obeyed, is salvific. Jesus shows us what we are meant to be. He shows us that we are created for a life of intimate relationship with God, and that that relationship makes us what we truly are. We know Jesus to be the Son of God because he is obedient to God, not because he has power. We know that, because he was willing to be obedient and to allow himself to be defined in relation to God, not on his own terms, he opens up a whole new kind of power, resurrection power. Resurrection power brings life out of death, creates community, opens up relationship, allows us to step into a place that we have not made or earned, but simply accepted, in gratitude. It is the place of God's children, standing by Jesus and knowing ourselves to be heirs, not servants.

The paradox that we see in Jesus is that it is *only* through service, through obedience, through accepting servant status that we come to be children, not slaves. Trying to get there under our own steam, relying always on our own powers, is going to keep us in slavery. It is to this question of our own obedience, and the corruptions of obedience, that we now turn, to an exploration of that paradoxical phrase, 'whose service is perfect freedom'.

# 3

## 'WHOSE SERVICE IS PERFECT FREEDOM'

Does the model of Jesus' obedience help us in the complex issues that we face nowadays? If we accept that obedience to God is part of the definition of what it is to be properly human, how do we work out, in particular circumstances, *how* to be obedient to God?

Before we start, it is worth summarizing one or two of the discoveries that we made in the last chapter.

- Jesus' obedience is to *God*, not to other people's vision of God.
- Jesus' obedience often looked like *disobedience* to others.
- Jesus' obedience was not always easy or clear.
- Jesus' obedience led to life for others.

How will any of this help us in the particularities of our own lives? Let us start with one of the most difficult and emotionally charged of areas: the relationship between men and women.

### 'The Husband is the Head of his Wife' – the New Testament Background

The New Testament has a number of passages that are hard for us to read today. I have heard a young woman stand up in chapel, read 1 Timothy 2:8–15, shut the Bible and announce 'This is *not* the Word of the Lord.' Many would sympathize.

So let us start with one or two details of background that might help to illuminate the situation addressed by these passages.

First of all, honesty compels me to admit that the Bible, as a whole, clearly believes in the subordination of women. It believes that there is a proper hierarchy in the world, and that *order*, which dictates how men relate to women, how humans relate to animals, and how the created relate to their Creator, is God-given.

The Bible does not invent this belief in the proper

submission of women to men. On the contrary, it is something to be found universally in the cultures in which the Bible comes into existence. In particular, it is important to note that it forms a natural part of the background world of the New Testament. Classical Greek and Roman writers take for granted as a biological fact that women are imperfect men, and that the proper form of the human being is male. All kinds of things follow from this, most notably that women are likely to lack the full rationality and force to be able to govern. This 'biology' that underpins a whole cultural attitude was supposed to be based on medical fact, not on philosophical and theological preconceptions.

In its benign form, this 'fact' gives men a responsibility for looking after women, and guiding them, using their greater rationality and stability for the protection of the weaker sex. That it also led to terrible abuse of women is clear from any reading of history. Though, equally, our own culture, which does not have that rationale, but has a rhetoric of 'equality', is not necessarily more protective of individual women.

Numerous examples from history show that there

were always exceptions to this as to every rule, and that there were women who governed, women whose rationality was recognized as the equal of a man's and so on.

This, then, is the background that the New Testament takes for granted. There is no point in blaming it for what we now know about biology, but which they did not and could not know.

Against this background, the statements on the relative positions of women and men can be seen to be an attempt on the part of early Christian leaders to produce a stable, respectable and sustainable Christian community. Husbands are always instructed to follow the best possible patterns for the treatment of their wives. Respect for their wives is enjoined at all times.

Writers like Elisabeth Schüssler Fiorenza have argued that this drive for respectability is modelled on the society in which the Church found itself, and so is a betrayal of the more radical teaching that it got from its founder.[1] Certainly, there are all kinds of signs within the New Testament that the instructions given in 1 Timothy or 1 Corinthians 11:3ff. were by no means universally obeyed. Indeed, if they could be taken for granted, it would not have been necessary to try and enforce them.

Women seem to have formed a significant element of Jesus' followers, and have played a substantial part in the continuing life of the Christian community ever since. No one has ever attempted to deny that women are called and saved just as men are and, more significantly, no one has ever attempted to say that God will not use women as his messengers, though women have traditionally had to work much harder than men to get their message heard and accepted.

This is all truly significant, but there is no point in trying to deny that, overall, the New Testament believes that women should be subordinate to men and, in particular, that wives should be subordinate to their husbands.

It is fascinating that the heart of the argument should revolve around this marriage relationship, rather than around the broader issues of how society should be ordered. This is partly because of the kind of community that Christianity was in those early years – small, domestic and lacking in any great influence. There was no point then in having political theories about the state, but there was a great deal of point in trying to get your own community into shape. Apart from anything else, to be well-ordered and not too obviously different in practice from your neighbours might save you from persecution. It might even make it less scary for others to join you.

But it is also, of course, true that general theories of how men and women should relate are often put to the test by the reality of how they actually relate. Whole cultures that have a theoretical belief in the authority of men also know of men who are wholly governed by their wives. It is under the day-to-day pressure of love, sex, caring for children, living together, that most of us discover what we actually believe about the proper relationships between men and women.

The writer of the letter to the Ephesians does not want to keep the proper relationship between women and men as a sociological discussion. He wants to ground it firmly in theology.

Wives, be subject to your husbands as you are to the Lord. For the husband is the head of the wife just as Christ is head of the church, the body of which he is the Saviour . . . . Husbands, love your wives, just as Christ loved the church and gave himself up for her . . . . This is a great mystery, and I am applying it to Christ and the church. (Ephesians 5:22–32)

This statement encourages us to think christo-logically about the question of the relationship between men and women in marriage. To each partner in the relationship, Christ is held up as the model.

Wives are to offer their husbands the obedience that they have learned to offer Christ. What kind of obedience is that? We have seen Christ calling women to be his followers, preaching the gospel to them, turning to them in his need, treating them, in other words, like real people, just as he treated men. We have seen, in all the history of Christianity, that Christ calls women to be obedient to the gospel, to preach it, teach it, suffer and die for it.

So this obedience that women offer to Christ is, indeed, an obedience that makes them free, adult, responsible. Obedience to Christ demands the most that you can be.

Might obedience to a husband carry with it the same expectations? That such an obedience will be stretching, but not distorting? That it will aim to make the wife a responsible partner in the gospel mission?

And what of the husband's part? If he is to give himself to the relationship as Christ does to us, what might that mean? We Christians are called to be 'the body of Christ'. As Teresa of Avila said, 'Christ has no hands on earth but my hands to do his bidding.' So Christ gives us partnership, responsibility, he trusts himself and his whole message about the Kingdom of God into our hands. Might a husband's duty to his wife meet such high expectations?

It is easy to be distracted by the apparent inequality of what is being asked of husbands and of wives in Ephesians, but if you take seriously the pattern that is implied by the reference to Christ, then what is involved is far less damaging but more demanding. *Both* partners have to model themselves on what they have learned through watching the obedience of Christ.

If Christ is followed as the pattern for both partners, Christian marriage might, potentially, create a place where God is obeyed, where men and women, wishing to honour and obey Christ in each other, create a human community that in some small part reflects the selfless and loving community of the Trinity.

It is central to what we have discovered in our study of Jesus' obedience that Jesus' distinctiveness is established through his relationship with the Father. He is not the Father, but the Son. So, in human community, relationships of obedience and respect ought to make each person more themselves. They should not be based on an attempt to make everyone in the same kind of mould, but, on the contrary, on a willingness on each person's part to discover what is their own distinctive nature and offer it for the enlargement of the rest.

You might also expect that, just as Jesus' willingness to be himself and not the Father opens up a place for us to be in communion with God, so human marriage that is trying to model itself on Jesus might open up a vision and experience of love and community that is a gift to others. In other words, the marriage relationship is not just meant to be good for those involved, but is also meant to be a metaphor of God's faithfulness and commitment for others.

Just as Jesus' obedience to the Father does not come without struggle, so human relating should not be expected to be plain sailing all the time. But the struggle we are talking about should be relational, not confrontational. It should not be about two egos asserting their rights, but about two people working out, sometimes painfully, how to make the sum of their relationship bigger than the parts. Implicit in this is a willingness to be vulnerable, a willingness to give up what seems dear and even essential to each one, for the greater good.

But also implicit is the knowledge that obedience can look like disobedience. Neither person in a marriage can just cite 'the rules' and expect obedience. Every call for submission or obedience, every piece of give and take, needs to be measured against the final goal of a marriage, which is to create a vision of Christ's love for the Church.

And how exactly does Christ love the Church? He calls it into being, he makes a space for it to live, he gives it enormous responsibility, combined with the promise of forgiveness, and he gives it himself.

So, finally, if Jesus is shown to be who he is by his

obedience to the Father, then we can be shown to be who we are by obedience to Christ. To acknowledge this kind of 'headship' may look like a diminution of freedom, if freedom is seen primarily in terms of the rights of one individual over against another. But if freedom is seen, instead, as being able to become who you are in relation to others, then we might have a model that can transform more than just marriage.

I am not trying to pretend that the New Testament is arguing for the equality of husband and wife in marriage. But in the proper rejection of obsolete models of dominance, we must not also reject what is actually being said by these hard biblical passages. What is *novel* is the extraordinary suggestion that the marriage relationship can be seen as a theological model. To start from marriage and see what that might mean for your concept first of the Church and then of God is very radical theology. It requires each married couple to take their relationship as seriously as that. Where these passages are just being used as anti-feminist hammers, the chance for a real experience of God is lost.

## *Learning Obedience*

What comes clearly out of an exploration of Jesus' obedience and the proper relationship between women and men in marriage is that the kind of obedience we are looking for is not a matter of rules. In a way, rules would be easier, because you would know whether or not you are keeping them. But most of us, most of the time, even if we are trying to want to be obedient to God, are not very sure when we have achieved it.

There are, of course, people who seem to have a direct line to God, and who have a clear and detailed sense of what God is asking in every circumstance of their lives. But, in my experience, that is the exception, not the rule. After all, the New Testament record suggests that even Jesus had occasions when he was uncertain what God was asking him to do.

If all that we have been arguing above has any coherence, then one or two practical things might follow. Perhaps the most important is a shift in our understanding of *disobedience* and its consequences. If obedience is primarily about being who we are meant to be in relation to God, then disobedience is a failure of relation and a diminution of ourselves. But it is not the end of the road. This kind of model of obedience lives in a world in which we know the proper claims God makes on us, so that even when we cannot fulfil them, we know whose kingdom we live in. The very fact that we think of our failure as 'disobedience' acknowledges our desire for obedience.

But although there are times when we actively do what we know to be wrong, what we know will fracture our relationship with God, and diminish the human community we long for, there are far more times when we simply do not know whether we are doing God's will or not. How does the exploration of obedience help us here?

Most of us have to learn obedience through a lifetime's study of the God we are trying to obey. The best way to know the will of God is to read the Bible, pray and try to follow Christ. This is best done in the company of others, because it is so easy to deceive oneself, and other people's differences can be a useful corrective to our smug belief that we have found a God in our own image.

That may sound like hard and discouraging work,

and sometimes it will be so. But there is hope. By even trying to obey God, however much we fail, we are acknowledging that we owe him obedience. In other words, we are acknowledging that he is the King, and that means that, even in our failures, we are helping to make the Kingdom of God real.

And the other great source of hope is that God asks for our obedience in order to give us freedom. To serve God in trying to imitate the Son, we become what we are meant to be, fully human, in the image of our creator. To serve anything else is to fall back into slavery, but to serve the living God is perfect freedom.

## Conclusion

Christian obedience, I have suggested, is nothing like the unquestioning allegiance to authority that hands over the individual will and moral judgement into the keeping of others. On the contrary, it is a hard and continuing learning to be more and more truthfully what you are meant to be in relation to others and to God.

This obedience is 'perfect freedom' precisely

because it challenges us not be enslaved by anything less than God. Nothing and nobody else has the right to ask us to change in order to be in their image. But God does indeed ask us to become more and more like him, as he reveals himself in Christ. Jesus Christ, fully obedient to the Father, is also so free that neither sin nor death can hold him.

This kind of obedience, then, offers us the freedom to be what we are created for – people in God's image, as Christ is. In the name of this obedience, Christians have had to challenge all kinds of other powers and authorities, from the time of the Roman Empire onwards. Obedience is by no means passive, and it may be judged 'disobedient' by those who are using a different measure. Obedience may lead, as Christ's did, to the cross. But we know that Christ's obedience bought for us the chance of the freedom to be heirs, not slaves, in God's world, and it is possible that our obedience will help to show others the way into the perfect freedom of those who are obedient to God.

# NOTES

*Chapter 1*

1. *Jesus – God and Man*, SCM Press 1976, p. 339.

*Chapter 3*

1. Elisabeth Schüssler Fiorenza, *In Memory of Her*, SCM Press 1983.